THE OUTLINE OF KNOWLEDGE

EDITED BY

JAMES A. RICHARDS

DRAMA

VOLUME XVII

J. A. RICHARDS, INC.
NEW YORK

Typesetting, Paper, Printing, Binding and Cloth
BY THE KINGSPORT PRESS
Kingsport, Tenn.

CONTENTS

DRAMA

AGAMEMNON

(Aeschylus, the father of Greek tragedy, was born at Eleusis, 525 B.C. At an early age he began writing for the theatre, producing about seventy dramas of which only about seven survive. Among these are, "The Suppliants," "Seven Against Thebes," and "Agamemnon." Aeschylus was not only a writer but he also fought in the Grecian wars against Persia, being present at the famous battle of Marathon, Salamis, Artemisium, and Plataea. Being the greatest of Greek tragic poets, he differed from his rival Sophocles in that his plays deal with larger issues of fate, and his grandeur of conception. Tradition tells that he was warned he would meet death by a fall of a house and retiring to the fields he was killed by an eagle letting a tortoise fall on his bald head, 456 B.C.)

A LYRICO-DRAMATIC SPECTACLE

" Οἱ Τρώων μεν ὑπεξέφυγον στονόεσσαν ἀῦτὴν
'Εν νόστῳ δ' απόλοντο κακῆς ἰστητι γυναικσσ."

"Greeks that 'scaped the Trojan war-cry, and the wailing battle-field,
But home returning basely perished by a wicked woman's guile."

HOMER, *Odys.* xi. 383-4.

PERSONS

Watchman.
Chorus of Argive Elders.
Clytemnestra, Wife of Agamemnon.
Herald.
Agamemnon, King of Argos and Mycenæ.
Cassandra, a Trojan Prophetess, Daughter of Priam.
Ægisthus, Son of Thyestes.
Scene—*The Royal Palace in Argos.*

INTRODUCTORY REMARKS

OF all that rich variety of Epic materials with which the early minstrel-literature of Greece supplied the drama of a future age, there was no more notable cycle among the ancients than that which went by the popular name of Νόστοι, or the *Returns;* comprehending an account of the adventures that befell the various Hellenic heroes of the Trojan war in their return home. To this cycle, in its most general acceptation, the Odyssey itself belongs; though the name of Νόστοι, according to the traditions of the ancient grammarians, is more properly confined to a legendary Epic, composed by an old poet, Agias of Troezene, of which the return of Agamemnon and Menelaus forms the principal subject. Of this Epos the grammarian Proclus gives us the following abstract:—

"Athena raises a strife between Agamemnon and Menelaus concerning their voyage homeward. Agamemnon remains behind, in order to pacify the wrath of Athena; but Diomede and Nestor depart, and return in safety to their own country. After them Menelaus sails, and arrives with five ships in Egypt; the rest of his vessels having been lost in a storm. Meanwhile, Calchas and Leonteus and Polypœtes go to Colophon, and celebrate the funeral obsequies of Tiresias, who had died there. There is then introduced the shade of Achilles appearing to Agamemnon, and warning him of the dangers that he was about to encounter. Then follows a storm as the fleet is passing the Capharean rocks, at the south promontory of Eubœa, on which occasion the Locrian Ajax is destroyed by the wrath of Athena, whom he had offended. Neoptolemus, on the other hand, under the protection of Thetis, makes his way overland through Thrace (where he encounters Ulysses in Maronea), to his native country, and proceeding to the country of the Molossi, is there recognized by his grandfather, the aged Peleus, the father of Achilles. The poem then concludes with an account of the murder of Agamemnon by Ægisthus and Clytemnestra, of the revenge taken on her by Orestes and Pylades, and of the return of Menelaus to Lacedæmon."

The last sentence of this curious notice contains the Epic germ of which the famous trilogy—the Agamemnon, the Choephorœ, and the Eumenides of Æschylus—the three plays contained in the present volume, present the dramatic expansion. The celebrity of the legends with regard to the return of the mighty Atridan arose naturally from

2 DRAMA

the prominent situation in which he stood as the admiral of the famous
thousand-masted fleet; and, besides, the passage from the old
Troezenian minstrel just quoted, is sufficiently attested by various
passages—some of considerable length—in the Odyssey, which will
readily present themselves to the memory of those who are familiar
with the productions of the great Ionic Epopœist. In the very opening of that poem, for instance, occur the following remarkable lines:—

"Strange, O strange, that mortal men immortal gods will still be
   blaming,
  Saying that the source of evil lies with us; while they, in sooth,
  More than Fate would have infatuate with sharp sorrows pierce
   themselves!
Thus even now Ægisthus, working sorrow more than Fate would
   have,
  The Atridan's wife hath wedded, and himself returning slain,
  Knowing well the steep destruction that awaits him; for ourselves
  Sent the sharp-eyed Argus-slayer, Hermes, to proclaim our will,
  That nor him he dare to murder, nor his wedded wife to woo.
  Thus spoke Hermes well and wisely; but the reckless wit, Ægisthus,
  Moved he not; full richly therefore now thy folly's fine thou payest."

And the same subject is reverted to in the Third Book (v. 194),
where old Nestor, in Pylos, gives an account to Telemachus, first of
his own safe return, and then of the fate of the other Greeks, so far
as he knew; and, again, in the Fourth Book (v. 535) where Menelaus
is informed of his brother's sad fate (slain "like a bull in a stall") by
the old prophetic Proteus, the sea harlequin of the African coast;
and, also, in the Eleventh Book (v. 405), where Ulysses, in Hades,
hears the sad recital from the injured shade of the royal Atridan
himself.

The tragic events by which Agamemnon and his family have ac-
quired such a celebrity in the epic and dramatic annals of Greece, are
but the sequel and consummation of a series of similar events com-
mencing with the great ancestor of the family; all which hang together in the chain of popular tradition by the great moral principal
so often enunciated in the course of these dramas, that sin has always
a tendency to propagate its like, and a root of bitterness once planted
in a family, will grow up and branch out luxuriantly, till, in the fulness
of time, it bears those bloody blossoms, and fruits of perdition that are
its natural product. The guilty ancestor, in the present case, is the
well-known Tantalus, the peculiar style of whose punishment in the
infernal regions has been stereotyped, for the modern memory, in
the shape of one of the most common and most expressive words
in the English language. Tantalus, a son of Jove, a native of Sipylos

in Phrygia, and who had been admitted to the table of the gods, thinking it a small matter to know the divine counsels, if he did not, at the same time, gratify his vanity by making a public parade of his knowledge before profane ears, was punished in the pit of Tartarus by those tortures of ever reborn and never gratified desire which every schoolboy knows. His son, Pelops, an exile from his native country, comes with great wealth to Pisa; and having, by stratagem, won, in a chariot race, Hippodamia, the daughter of Oernomaus, king of that place, himself succeeded to the kingdom, and became so famous, according to the legend, as to lend a new name to the southern peninsula of Greece which was the theatre of his exploits. In his career also, however, the traces of blood are not wanting, which soil so darkly the path of his no less famous descendants. Pelops slew Myrtilus, the charioteer by whose aid he had won the race that was the beginning of his greatness; and it was the Fury of this Myrtilus— or "his blood crying to Heaven," as in Christian style we should express it—that, according to one poet (Eurip. Orest. 981), gave rise to the terrible retributions of blood by which the history of the Pelopidan family is marked. Of Pelops, according to the common account, Atreus and Thyestes were the sons. These having murdered their stepbrother, Chrysippus, were obliged to flee for safety to Mycenæ, in Argolis, where, in the course of events, they afterwards established themselves, and became famous for their wealth and for their crimes. The bloody story of these hostile brothers commences with the seduction, by Thyestes, of Aerope, the wife of Atreus; in revenge for which insult, Atreus recalls his banished brother, and, pretending reconciliation, offers that horrid feast of human flesh—the blood of the children to the lips of the father—from which the sun turned away his face in horror. The effect of this deed of blood was to entail, between the two families of Thyestes and Atreus, a hereditary hostility, the fruits of which appeared afterwards in the person of Ægisthus, the son of the former, who is found, in this first play of the trilogy, engaged with Clytemnestra in a treacherous plot to revenge his father's wrongs, by the murder of his uncle's son.

Agamemnon, the son, or, according to a less common account (for which see Schol. ad Iliad II. 249), the grandson of Atreus, being distinguished above the other Hellenic princes for wealth and power, was either by special election appointed, or by that sort of irregular kingship common among half-civilized nations, allowed to conduct the famous expedition against Troy that in early times foreshadowed the conquests of Alexander the Great, and the influence of the Greek language and letters in the East. Such a distant expedition as this, like the crusades in the middle ages, was not only a natural living Epos in itself, but would necessarily give rise to that intense glow of popular sympathy, and that excited state of the popular imagination, which enable the wandering poets of the people to make the best poetic use of the various dramatic incidents that the realities of a highly potentiated history present. Accordingly we find, in the very outset of the expedition, the fleet, storm-bound in the harbour of Aulis, opposite Eubœa, enabled to pursue its course, under good omens, only by the sacrifice of the fairest daughter of the chief. This event—a sad memorial of the barbarous practice of human sacrifice, even among the polished Greeks—formed the subject of a special play, perhaps a trilogic series of plays, by Æschylus. This performance, however, has been unfortunately lost; and we can only imagine what it may have been by the description in the opening chorus of the present play, and by the beautiful, though certainly far from Æschylean, tragedy of Euripides. For our present purpose, it is sufficient to note that, in the Agamemnon, special reference is made to the sacrifice of Iphigenia, both as an unrighteous deed on the part of the father, for which some retribution was naturally to be expected, and as the origin of a special grudge in the mind of the mother, which she afterwards gratifies by the murder of her husband.

As to that deed of blood itself, and its special adaptation for dramatic purposes, there can be no doubt; as little that Æschylus has used his materials in the present play in a fashion that satisfies the highest demands both of lyric and dramatic poetry, as executed by the first masters of both. The calm majesty and modest dignity of the much-tried monarch; the cool self-possession, and the smooth front of specious politeness that mark the character of the royal murderess: the obstreperous bullying of the cowardly braggart, who does the deed with his heart, not with his hand; the half-wild, half-tender ravings of the horror-haunted Trojan prophetess; these together contain a combination of highly wrought dramatic elements, such as is scarcely excelled even in the all-embracing pages of our own Shakespere. As far removed from common-place are the lyrical —in Æschylus never the secondary—elements of the piece. The sublime outbreak of Cassandra's prophetic horror is, as the case demanded, made to exhibit itself as much under the lyric as in the declamatory form; while the other choral parts, remarkable for length and variety, are marked not only by that mighty power of intense moral feeling which is so peculiarly Æschylean, but by the pictorial beauty and dramatic reality that distinguish the workmanship of a great lyric master from that of the vulgar dealer in inflated sentiment and sonorous sentences.

AGAMEMNON

Watch.—I pray the gods a respite from these toils,
    This long year's watch that, dog-like, I have kept,
    High on the Atridan's battlements, beholding
    The nightly council of the stars, the circling
    Of the celestial signs, and those bright regents,
    High-swung in ether, that bring mortal men
    Summer and winter. Here I watch the torch,
    The appointed flame that wings a voice from Troy,
    Telling of capture; thus I serve her hopes,
    The masculine-minded who is sovereign here,
    And when night-wandering shades encompass round
    My dew-sprent dreamless couch (for fear doth sit
    In slumber's chair, and holds my lids apart),
    I chaunt some dolorous ditty, making song,
    Sleep's substitute, surgeon my nightly care,
    And the misfortunes of this house I weep,
    Not now, as erst, by prudent counsels swayed.
    Oh! soon may the wished for sign relieve my toils,
    Thrice-welcome herald, gleaming through the night!

(The beacon is seen shining)

All hail thou cresset of the dark! fair gleam
    Of day through midnight shed, all hail! bright father
    Of joy and dance, in Argos, hail! all hail!
    Hillo! hilloa!
    I will go tell the wife of Agamemnon
    To shake dull sleep away, and lift high-voiced
    The jubilant shout well-omened, to salute
    This welcome beacon; if, indeed, old Troy
    Hath fallen—as flames this courier torch to tell.
    Myself will dance the prelude to this joy.
    My master's house hath had a lucky throw,
    And thrice six falls to me, thanks to the flame
    Soon may he see his home; and soon may I
    Carry my dear-loved master's hand in mine!
    The rest I whisper not, for on my tongue
    Is laid a seal. These walls, if they could speak,
    Would say strange things. Myself to those that know
    Am free of speech, to whoso knows not dumb.   (Exit.

5

Enter CHORUS *in procession. March time*

Nine years have rolled, the tenth is rolling,
Since the strong Atridan pair,
Menelaus and Agamemnon,
Sceptred kings by Jove's high grace,
With a host of sworn alliance,
With a thousand triremes rare,
With a righteous strong defiance,
Sailed for Troy. From furious breast
Loud they clanged the peal of battle;
Like the cry of vultures wild
O'er the lone paths fitful-wheeling,
With their plumy oarage oaring
Over the nest by the spoiler spoiled,
The nest dispeopled now and bare,
　　　Their long but fruitless care.
But the gods see it: some Apollo,
Pan or Jove, the wrong hath noted,
Heard the sharp and piercing cry
Of the startled birds, shrill-throated
　　　Tenants of the sky;
And the late-chastising Fury
Sent from above to track the spoiler,
　　　Hovers vengeful night.

Thus great Jove, the high protector
Of the hospitable laws,
'Gainst Alexander sends the Atridans,
Harnessed in a woman's cause,
The many-lorded fair.
Toils on toils shall come uncounted,
　　　(Jove hath willed it so);
Limb-outwearying hard endeavour,
Where the strong knees press the dust,
Where the spear-shafts split and shiver,
　　　Trojan and Greek shall know.
But things are as they are: the chain
Of Fate doth bind them; sighs are vain,
Tears, libations, fruitless flow,
To divert from purposed ire
The powers whose altars know no fire.
But we behind that martial train
　　　Inglorious left remain,
Old and frail, and feebly leaning

Strength as of childhood on a staff.
Yea! even as life's first unripe marrow
In the tender bones are we,
From war's harsh service free.
For hoary Eld, life's leaf up-shrunken,
Totters, his three-footed way
Feebly feeling, weak as childhood,
Like a dream that walks by day.
But what is this? what wandering word,
Clytemnestra queen, hath reached thee?
What hast seen? or what hast heard
That from street to street swift flies
Thy word, commanding sacrifice?
All the altars of all the gods
That keep the city, gods supernal,
Gods Olympian, gods infernal,
Gods of the Forum, blaze with gifts;
Right and left the flame mounts high,
Spiring to the sky,
With the gentle soothings cherished
Of the oil that knows no malice,
And the sacred cake that smokes
From the queen's chamber in the palace.
What thou canst and may'st, declare;
Be the healer of the care
That bodes black harm within me; change it
To the bright and hopeful ray,
Which from altar riseth, chasing
From the heart the sateless sorrow
That eats vexed life away.

The CHORUS, *having now arranged themselves into a regular band
in the middle of the Orchestra, sing the First* CHORAL HYMN

STROPHE

I'll voice the strain. What though the arm be weak
That once was strong,
The suasive breath of Heaven-sent memories stirs
The old man's breast with song.
My age hath virtue left
To sing what fateful omens strangely beckoned
The twin kings to the fray,
What time to Troy concentuous marched
The embattled Greek array.
Jove's swooping bird, king of all birds, led on

The kings of the fleet with spear and vengeful hand:
By the way-side from shining seats serene,
Close by the palace, on the spear-hand seen,
    To eagles flapped the air,
One black, the other silver-tipt behind,
And with keen talons seized a timorous hare,
    Whose strength could run no more,
Itself, and the live burden which it bore.
    Sing woe and well-a-day! But still
    May the good omens shame the ill.

ANTISTROPHE

The wise diviner of the host beheld,
    And knew the sign;
The hare-devouring birds with diverse wings
    Typed the Atridan pair,
    The diverse-minded kings;
And thus the fate he chaunted:—Not in vain
    Ye march this march to-day;
    Old Troy shall surely fall, but not
    Till moons on moons away
Have lingering rolled. Rich stores by labour massed
Clean-sweeping Fate shall plunder. Grant the gods,
While this strong bit for Troy we forge with gladness,
No heavenly might in jealous wrath o'ercast
    Our mounting hope with sadness.
For the chaste Artemis a sore grudge nurses
Against the kings; Jove's winged hounds she curses,
    The fierce war-birds that tore
The fearful hare, with the young brood it bore.
    Sing woe and well-a-day! but still
    May the good omens shame the ill.

EPODE

The lion's fresh-dropt younglings, and each whelp
That sucks wild milk, and through the forest roves,
Live not unfriended; them the fair goddess loves,
    And lends her ready help.
The vision of the birds shall work its end
In bliss, but dashed not lightly with black bane;
I pray thee, Pæan, may she never send
Contrarious blasts dark-lowering, to detain
    The Argive fleet.

Ah! ne'er may she desire to feast her eyes
On an unblest unholy sacrifice,
From festal use abhorrent, mother of strife,
And sundering from her lawful lord the wife.
Stern-purposed waits the child-avenging wrath
        About the fore-doomed halls,
Weaving dark wiles, while with sure-memoried sting
        Fury to Fury calls.
Thus hymned the seer, the doom, in dubious chaunt
Bliss to the chiefs dark-mingling with the bane,
      From the way-haunting birds; and we
        Respondent to the strain,
      Sing woe and well-a-day! but still
      May the good omens shame the ill.

STROPHE I

      Jove, or what other name
The god that reigns supreme delights to claim,
Him I invoke; him of all powers that be,
        Alone I find,
Who from this bootless load of doubt can free
      My labouring mind.

ANTISTROPHE I

      Who was so great of yore,
With all-defiant valour brimming o'er,
Is mute; and who came next by a stronger arm
        Thrice-vanquished fell;
But thou hymn victor Jove: so in thy heart
      His truth shall dwell.

STROPHE II

For Jove doth teach men wisdom, sternly wins
To virtue by the tutoring of their sins;
Yea! drops of torturing recollection chill
The sleeper's heart; 'gainst man's rebellious will
      Jove works the wise remorse:
Dread Powers, on awful seats enthroned, compel
      Our hearts with gracious force.

ANTISTROPHE II

The elder chief, the leader of the ships,
Heard the dire doom, nor dared to ope his lips
Against the seer, and feared alone to stand
'Gainst buffeting fate, what time the Chalcian strand
     Saw the vexed Argive masts
In Aulis tides hoarse-refluent, idly chained
     By the fierce Borean blasts;

STROPHE III

Blasts from Strymon adverse braying,
Harbour-vexing, ship-delaying,
Snapping cables, shattering oars,
Wasting time, consuming stores,
With vain-wandering expectation,
And with long-drawn slow vexation
     Wasting Argive bloom.
At length the seer forth-clanged the doom,
A remedy strong to sway the breeze,
And direful Artemis to appease,
     But to the chiefs severe:
The Atridans with their sceptres struck the ground,
     Nor could restrain the tear.

ANTISTROPHE III

Then spake the elder. To deny,
   How hard! still harder to comply!
My daughter dear, my joy, my life,
To slay with sacrificial knife,
And with life's purple-gushing tide,
Imbrue a father's hand, beside
     The altar of the gods.
This way or that is ill: for how
Shall I despise my federate vow?
How leave the ships? That all conspire
     Thus hotly to desire
The virgin's blood—wind-soothing sacrifice—
     Is the gods' right. So be it.

STROPHE IV

Thus to necessity's harsh yoke he bared
His patient neck. Unblissful blew the gale
     That turned the father's heart

To horrid thoughts unholy, thoughts that dared
The extreme of daring. Sin from its primal spring
Mads the ill-counsell'd heart, and arms the hand
      With reckless strength. Thus he
Gave his own daughter's blood, his life, his joy,
To speed a woman's war, and consecrate
      His ships for Troy.

ANTISTROPHE IV

In vain with prayers, in vain she beats dull ears
With a father's name; the war-delighting chiefs
      Heed not her virgin years.
The father stood; and when the priests had prayed
Take her, he said; in her loose robes enfolden,
Where prone and spent she lies, so lift the maid;
      Even as a kid is laid,
So lay her on the altar; with dumb force
Her beauteous mouth gag, lest it breathe a voice
      Of curse to Argos.

STROPHE V

And as they led the maid, her saffron robe
Sweeping the ground, with pity-moving dart
      She smote each from her eye,
Even as a picture beautiful, fain to speak,
But could not. Well that voice they knew of yore;
      Oft at her father's festive board,
With gallant banqueters ringed cheerly round,
      The virgin strain they heard
      That did so sweetly pour
Her father's praise, whom Heaven had richly crowned
      With bounty brimming o'er.

ANTISTROPHE V

The rest I know not, nor will vainly pry;
But Calchas was a seer not wont to lie.
      Justice doth wait to teach
Wisdom by suffering. Fate will have its way.
The quickest ear is pricked in vain to-day,
      To catch to-morrow's note. What boots
To forecast woe, which, on no wavering wing,
      The burden'd hour shall bring.
      But we, a chosen band,

Left here sole guardians of the Apian land,
    Pray Heaven, all good betide!

Enter CLYTEMNESTRA

Chorus.—Hail Clytemnestra! honour to thy sceptre!
    When her lord's throne is vacant, the wife claims
    His honor meetly. Queen, if thou hast heard
    Good news, or to the hope of good that shall be,
    With festal sacrifice dost fill the city,
    I fain would know; but nothing grudge thy silence.
Clytem.—Bearing blithe tidings, saith the ancient saw,
    Fair Morn be gendered from boon mother Night!
    News thou shalt hear beyond thy topmost hope;
    The Greeks have ta'en old Priam's city.
Chorus.   How!
    Troy taken! the word drops from my faithless ear.
Clytem.—The Greeks have taken Troy. Can I speak plainer?
Chorus.—Joy o'er my heart creeps, and provokes the tear.
Clytem.—Thine eye accuses thee that thou art kind.
Chorus.—What warrant of such news? What certain sign?
Clytem.—Both sign and seal, unless some god deceive me.
Chorus.—Dreams sometimes speak; did suasive visions move thee?
Clytem.—Where the soul sleeps, and the sense slumbers, there
    Shall the wise ask for reasons?
Chorus.   Ever swift
    Though wingless, Fame, with tidings fair hath cheered thee.
Clytem.—Thou speak'st as one who mocks a simple girl.
Chorus.—Old Troy is taken? how?—when did it fall?
Clytem.—The self-same night that mothers this to-day.
Chorus.—But how? what stalwart herald ran so fleetly?
Clytem.—Hephætus. He from Ida shot the spark;
    And flaming straightway leapt the courier fire
    From height to height; to the Hermæan rock
    Of Lemnos, first from Ida; from the isle
    The Athoan steep of mighty Jove received
    The beaming beacon; thence the forward strength
    Of the far-travelling lamp strode gallantly
    Athwart the broad sea's back. The flaming pine
    Rayed out a golden glory like the sun,
    And winged the message of Macistus' watch-tower.
    There the wise watchman, guiltless of delay,
    Lent to the sleepless courier further speed;
    And the Messapian station hailed the torch
    Far-beaming o'er the floods of the Eurípus.

There the grey health lit the responsive fire,
Speeding the portioned message; waxing strong,
And nothing dulled across Asopus' plain
The flame swift darted like the twinkling moon,
And on Cithæron's rocky heights awaked
A new receiver of the wandering light.
The far-sent ray, by the faithful watch not spurned,
With bright addition journeying, bounded o'er
Gorgópus' lake and Ægiplanctus' mount,
Weaving the chain unbroken. Hence it spread
Not scant in strength, a mighty beard of flame,
Flaring across the headlands that look down
On the Saronic gulf. Speeding its march,
It reached the neighbour-station of our city,
Arachne's rocky steep; and thence the halls
Of the Atridæ recognised the signal,
Light not unfathered by Idæan fire.
Such the bright train of my torch-bearing heralds,
Each from the other fired with happy news,
And last and first was victor in the race
Such the fair tidings that my lord hath sent,
A sign that Troy hath fallen.

Chorus.—   And for its fall
    Our voice shall hymn the gods anon: meanwhile
    I'm fain to drink more wonder from thy words.

Clytem.—This day Troy fell. Methinks I see'st; a host
    Of jarring voices stirs the startled city,
    Like oil and acid, sounds that will not mingle,
    By natural hatred sundered. Thou may'st hear
    Shouts of the victor, with the dying groan,
    Battling, and captives' cry; upon the dead—
    Fathers and mothers, brothers, sisters, wives—
    The living fall—the young upon the old;
    And from enthralléd necks wail out their woe.
    Fresh from the fight, through the dark night the spoilers
    Tumultuous rush where hunger spurs them on,
    To feast on banquets never spread for them.
    The homes of captive Trojan chiefs they share
    As chance decides the lodgment; there secure
    From the cold night-dews and the biting frosts,
    Beneath the lordly roof, to their hearts' content
    They live, and through the watchless night prolong
    Sound slumbers. Happy if the native gods
    They reverence, and the captured altars spare,
    Themselves not captive led by their own folly!

May no unbridled lust of unjust gain
Master their hearts, no reckless rash desire!
Much toil yet waits them. Having turned the goal,
The course's other half they must mete out,
Ere home receive them safe. Their ships must brook
The chances of the sea; and, these being scaped,
If they have sinned the gods their own will claim,
And vengeance wakes till blood shall be atoned.
I am a woman; but mark thou well my words;
I hint the harm; but with no wavering scale,
Prevail the good! I thank the gods who gave me
Rich store of blessings, richly to enjoy.
Chorus.—Woman, thou speakest wisely as a man,
And kindly as thyself. But having heard
The certain signs of Agememnon's coming,
Prepare we now to hymn the gods; for surely
With their strong help we have not toiled in vain.

O regal Jove! O blessed Night!
Thou hast won thee rich adornments,
Thou hast spread thy shrouding meshes
O'er the towers of Priam. Ruin
Whelms the young, the old. In vain
Shall they strive to o'erleap the snare,
And snap the bondsman's galling chain,
    In woe retrieveless lost.
Jove, I fear thee, just protector
Of the wrong'd host's sacred rights;
Thou didst keep thy bow sure bent
'Gainst Alexander; not before
The fate-predestined hour, and not
Beyond the stars, with idle aim,
    Thy cunning shaft was shot.

CHORAL HYMN

STROPHE I

The hand of Jove hath smote them; thou
        May'st trace it plainly;
What the god willed, behold it now
        Not purposed vainly!
The gods are blind and little caring,
So one hath said, to mark the daring
Of men, whose graceless foot hath ridden
O'er things to human touch forbidden.

Godless who said so; sons shall rue
    Their parents' folly,
Who flushed with wealth, with insolence flown,
The sober bliss of man outgrown,
The tramp of Mars unchastened blew,
And stirred red strife without the hue
    Of justice wholly.
Live wiselier thou; not waxing gross
With gain, thou shalt be free from loss.
Weak is his tower, with pampering wealth
    On brief alliance
Who spurns great Justice' altar dread
    With damned defiance;
Him the deep hell shall claim, and shame
    His vain reliance.

ANTISTROPHE I

Self-will fell Até's daughter, still
    Fore-counselling ruin,
Shall spur him on resistless borne
    To his undoing.
Fined with sharp loss beyond repairing,
His mercy like a beacon flaring,
Shall shine to all. Like evil brass,
That tested shows a coarse black mass,
His deep distemper he shall show
    By dints of trial.
Even as a boy in wanton sport,
Chasing a bird to his own hurt,
And to the state's redeemless loss,
Whom, when he prays, the gods shall cross
    With sheer denial,
And sweep the lewd and lawless liver
From earth's fair memory for ever;
Thus to the Atridans' palace came
    False Alexander,
And shared the hospitable board,
    A bold offender,
Filching his host's fair wife away
    To far Scamander.

STROPHE II

She went, and to the Argive city left
    Squadrons shield-bearing,

Battle preparing.
Swords many-flashing
Oars many-plashing;
She went, destruction for her dowry bearing,
To the Sigean shore;
Light with swift foot she brushed the doorstead, daring
A deed undared before.
The prophets of the house loud wailing,
Cried with sorrow unavailing,
"Woe to the Atridans! woe!
The lofty palaces fallen low
The marriage and the marriage bed,
The steps once faithful, fond to follow
There where the faithful husband led!"
He silent stood in sadness, not in wrath,
His own eye scarce believing,
As he followed her flight beyond the path
Of the sea-wave broadly heaving.
And phantoms sway each haunt well known,
Which the lost loved one went to own,
And the statued forms that look from their seats
With a cold smile serenely,
He loathes to look on; in his eye
Pines Aphrodité leanly.

ANTISTROPHE II

In vain he sleeps; for in the fretful night
Shapes of fair seeming
Flit through his dreaming,
Soothing him sweetly,
Leaving him fleetly
Of bliss all barren. The shape fond fancy weaves him
His eager grasp would keep,
In vain; it cheats the hand; and leaves him, sweeping
Swift o'er the paths of sleep.
These sorrows pierce the Atridan chiefs,
And, worse than these, their private griefs,
But general Greece that to the fray
Sent her thousands, mourns to-day;
And Grief stout-hearted at each door
Sits to bear the burden sore
Of dreadful news from the Trojan shore.
Ah! many an Argive heart to-day
Is pricked with wail and mourning,

Knowing how many went to Troy,
From Troy how few returning!
The mothers of each house shall wait
To greet their sons at every gate;
But, alas! not men, but dust of men
    Each sorrowing house receiveth,
The urn in which the fleshly case
    Its cindered ruin leaveth.

STROPHE III

For Mars doth market bodies, and for gold
Gives dust, and in the battle of the bold
    Holds the dread scales of Fate.
Burnt cinders, a light burden, but to friends
    A heavy freight,
He sends from Troy; the beautiful vase he sends
With dust, for hearts, well lined, on which descends
    The frequent tear.
And friends do wait their praise; this here
Expert to wield the pointed spear,
And this who cast his life away,
Nobly in ignoble fray,
    For a strange woman's sake.
    And in their silent hearts hate burns;
        Against the kings
    The moody-muttered grudge creeps forth,
        And points its stings.
Others they mourn who 'neath Troy's wall
    Entombed, dark sleep prolong,
Low pressed beneath the hostile sod,
    The beautiful, the strong!

ANTISTROPHE III

O hard to bear, when evil murmurs fly,
Is a nation's hate; unblest on whom doth lie
    A people's curse!
My heart is dark, in my fear-procreant brain
    Bad begets worse.
For not from heaven the gods behold in vain
Hands red with slaughter. The black-mantled train
    Who watch and wait,
    In their own hours shall turn to bane
    The bliss that grew from godless gain.

The mighty man with heart elate
Shall fall; even as the sightless shades,
The great man's glory fades.
Sweet to the ear is the popular cheer
  Forth billowed loudly;
But the bolt from on high shall blast his eye
  That looketh proudly.
Be mine the sober bliss, and far
From fortune's high-strung rapture;
Not capturing others, may I never
See my own city's capture!

EPODE

Swift-winged with thrilling note it came,
The blithe news from the courier-flame;
But whether true and witnessed well,
Or if some god hath forged a lie,
  What tongue can tell?
Who is so young, so green of wit,
That his heart should blaze with a fever fit,
At a tale of this fire-courier's telling,
When a new rumour swiftly swelling,
May turn him back to dole? To lift the note
Of clamorous triumph ere the fight be fought,
  Is a light chance may fitly fall,
  Where women wield the spear
A wandering word by woman's fond faith sped
  Swells and increases,
But with dispersion swift a woman's tale
  Is lost and ceases.

Enter CLYTEMNESTRA

Soon shall we know if the light-bearing lamps
And the bright signals of the fiery changes
Spake true or, dream-like, have deceived our senses
With smiling semblance. For, behold, there comes,
Beneath the outspread olive's branchy shade,
A herald from the beach; and thirsty dust,
Twin-sister of the clay, attests his speed.
Not voiceless he, nor with the smoking flame
Of mountain pine will bring uncertain news.
His heraldry gives increase to our joy,
Or—but to speak ill-omened words I shun;—
May fair addition fair beginning follow!

Chorus.—Whoso fears evil where no harm appears,
    Reap first himself the fruit of his own fears.

Enter HERALD

Hail Argive land! dear fatherland, all hail!
This tenth year's light doth shine on my return!
And now this one heart's hope from countless wrecks
I save! Scarce hoped I e'er to lay my bones
Within the tomb, where dearest dust is stored.
I greet thee, native land! thee, shining sun!
Thee, the land's Sovereign, Jove! thee, Pythian King,
Shooting no more thy swift-winged shafts against us.
Enough on red Scamander's banks we knew
Thee hostile; now our saviour-god be thou,
Apollo, and our healer from much harm!
And you, all gods that guide the chance of fight,
I here invoke; and thee, my high protector,
Loved Hermes, of all heralds most revered.
And you, all heroes that sent forth our hosts,
Bring back, I pray, our remnant with good omens.
O kingly halls! O venerated seats!
O dear-loved roofs, and ye sun-fronting gods,
If ever erst, now on this happy day,
With these bright-beaming eyes, duly receive
Your late returning king; for Agamemnon
Comes, like the sun, a common joy to all.
Greet him with triumph, as beseems the man,
Who with the mattock of justice-bringing Jove
Hath dug the roots of Troy, hath made its altars
Things seen no more, its towering temples razed,
And caused the seed of the whole land to perish.
Such yoke on Ilium's haughty neck the elder
Atridan threw, a king whom gods have blessed
And men revere, 'mongst mortal worthy most
Of honor; now nor Paris, nor in the bond
Partner'd with him, old Troy more crime may boast
Than penalty; duly in the court of fight,
In the just doom of rape and robbery damned,
His pledge is forfeited; his hand hath reaped
Clean bare the harvest of all bliss from Troy.
Doubly they suffer for a double crime.
Chorus.—Hail soldier herald, how farest thou?
Herald.—   Right well!
    So well that I could bless the gods and die.
Chorus.—Doubtless thy love of country tried thy heart?

Herald.—To see these shores I weep for every joy.

Chorus.—And that soul-sickness sweetly held thee?

Herald.—   How?
 Instruct my wit to comprehend thy words.

Chorus.—Smitten with love of them that much loved thee.

Herald.—Say'st thou? loved Argos us as we loved Argos?

Chorus.—Ofttimes we sorrowed from a sunless soul.

Herald.—How so? Why should the thought of the host have
  clouded
 Thy soul with sadness?

Chorus.—   Sorrow not causeless came;
 But I have learned to drug all woes by silence.

Herald.—Whom should'st thou quail before, the chiefs away?

Chorus.—I could have used thy phrase, and wished to die.

Herald.—Die now, an' thou wilt, for joy! The rolling years
 Have given all things a prosperous end, though some
 Were hard to bear; for who, not being a god,
 Can hope to live long years of bliss unbroken?
 A weary tale it were to tell the tithe
 Of all our hardships; toils by day, by night,
 Harsh harbourage, hard hammocks, and scant sleep.
 No sun without new troubles, and new groans,
 Shone on our voyage; and when at length we landed,
 Our woes were doubled; 'neath the hostile walls,
 On marshy meads night-sprinkled by the dews,
 We slept, our clothes rotted with drenching rain,
 And like wild beasts with shaggy-knotted hair.
 Why should I tell bird-killing winter's sorrows,
 Long months of suffering from Idean snows,
 Then summer's scorching heat, when noon beheld
 The waveless sea beneath the windless air
 In sleep diffused; these toils have run their hour.
 The dead care not to rise; their roll our grief
 Would muster o'er in vain; and we who live
 Vainly shall fret at the cross strokes of fate.
 Henceforth to each harsh memory of the past
 Farewell! we who survive this long-drawn war
 Have gains to count that far outweigh the loss.
 Well may we boast in the face of the shining sun,
 O'er land and sea our winged tidings wafting,
 The Achæan host hath captured Troy; and now
 On the high temples of the gods we hang
 These spoils, a shining grace, there to remain
 An heritage for ever. These things to hear
 Shall men rejoice, and with fair praises laud

The state and its great generals, laud the grace
Of Jove the Consummator. I have said.
Chorus.—I own thy speech the conqueror; for a man
   Can never be too old to learn good news,
   And though thy words touch Clytemnestra most,
   Joy to the Atridan's halls is wealth to me.
Clytem.—I lifted first the shout of jubilee,
   Then when the midnight sign of the courier fire
   Told the deep downfall of the captured Troy;
   But one then mocked my faith, that I believed
   The fire-sped message in so true a tale.
   'Tis a light thing to buoy a woman's heart
   With hopeful news, they cried; and with these words
   They wildered my weak wit. And yet I sped
   The sacrifice, and raised the welcoming shout
   In woman's wise, and at a woman's word
   Forthwith from street to street uprose to the gods
   Well-omened salutations, and glad hymns,
   Lulling the fragrant incense-feeding flame.
   What needs there more? The event has proved me right,
   Himself—my lord—with his own lips shall speak
   The weighty tale; myself will go make ready
   With well-earned honour to receive the honoured.
   What brighter bliss on woman's lot may beam,
   Than when a god gives back her spouse from war,
   To ope the gates of welcome. Tell my husband,
   To his loved home, desired of all, to haste.
   A faithful wife, even as he left her, here
   He'll find expectant, like a watch-dog, gentle
   To him and his, to all that hate him harsh.
   The seals that knew his stamp, when hence he sailed,
   Unharmed remain, untouched: and for myself
   Nor praise nor blame from other man I know,
   No more than dyer's art can tincture brass.
Herald.—A boast like this, instinct with very truth,
   Comes from a noble lady without blame.
Chorus.—Wise words she spake, and words that need no com-
         ment
   To ears that understand. But say, good Herald,
   Comes Menelaus safe back from the wars,
   His kindly sway in Argos to resume?
Herald.—I cannot gloss a lie with fair pretence;
   The best told lie bears but a short-lived fruit.
Chorus.—Speak the truth plainly, if thou canst not pleasantly;
   These twain be seldom wedded; and here, alas!

They stand out sundered with too clear a mark.

Herald.—The man is vanished from the Achæan host,
He and his vessel. Thou hast heard the truth.

Chorus.—Sailed he from Ilium separate from the fleet?
Or did the tempest part him from his friends!

Herald.—Like a good marksman thou hast hit the mark,
In one short sentence summing many sorrows.

Chorus.—Alive is he or dead? What word hath reached you?
What wandering rumour from sea-faring men?

Herald.—This none can tell, save yon bright sun aloft,
That cherishes all things with his friendly light.

Chorus.—How came the storm on the fleet? or how was ended
The wrath of the gods?

Herald.—   Not well it suits to blot.
With black rehearsal this auspicious day.
Far from the honors of the blissful gods
Be grief's recital. When with gloomy visage
An ugly tale the herald's voice unfolds,
At once a general wound, and private grief,
An army lost, the sons of countless houses
Death-doomed by the double scourge so dear to Ares,
A twin-speared harm, a yoke of crimson slaughter:
A herald saddled with such woes may sing
A pæan to the Erinnyes. But I,
Who to this city blithe and prosperous
Brought the fair news of Agamemnon's safety,
How shall I mingle bad with good, rehearsing
The wintry wrath sent by the gods to whelm us?
Fire and the sea, sworn enemies of old,
Made friendly league to sweep the Achæan host
With swift destruction pitiless. Forth rushed
The tyrannous Thracian blasts, and wave chased wave,
Fierce 'neath the starless night, and ship on ship
Struck clashing; beak on butting beak was driven;
The puffing blast, the beat of boiling billows,
The whirling gulph (an evil pilot) wrapt them
In sightless death. And when the shining sun
Shone forth again, we see the Ægean tide
Strewn with the purple blossoms of the dead,
And wrecks of shattered ships. Us and our bark
Some god, no man, the storm-tost hull directing,
Hath rescued scathless, stealing us from the fray,
Or with a prayer begging our life from Fate.
Kind Fortune helmed us further, safely kept
From yeasty ferment in the billowy bay,

Nor dashed on far-ledged rocks. Thus having 'scaped
That ocean hell, scarce trusting our fair fortune,
We hailed the lucid day; but could we hope,
The chance that saved ourselves had saved our friends?
Our fearful hearts with thoughts of them we fed,
Far-labouring o'er the loosely-driving main.
And doubtless they, if yet live breath they breathe,
Deem so of us, as we must fear of them,
That they have perished. But I hope the best.
And first and chief expect ye the return
Of Menelaus. If the sun's blest ray
Yet looks on him, where he beholds the day
By Jove's devising, not yet willing wholly
To uproot the race of Atreus, hope may be
He yet returns. Thou hast my tale; and I
Have told the truth untinctured with a lie.   (Exit.

CHORAL HYMN

STROPHE I

Who gave her a name
So true to her fame?
Does a Providence rule in the fate of a word?
Sways there in heaven a viewless power
O'er the chance of the tongue in the naming hour?
Who gave her a name,
This daughter of strife, this daughter of shame,
The spear-wooed maid of Greece?
Helen the taker! 'tis plain to see
A taker of ships, a taker of men,
A taker of cities is she.
From the soft-curtained chamber of Hymen she fled,
By the breath of giant Zephyr sped,
And shield-bearing throngs in marshalled array
Hounded her flight o'er the printless way,
Where the swift-plashing oar
The fair booty bore
To whirling Simois' leafy shore,
And stirred the crimson fray.

ANTISTROPHE I

For the gods sent a bride,
Kin but not kind,
Ripe with the counsel of wrath to Troy,

In the fulness of years, the offender to prove,
And assert the justice of Jove;
For great Jove is lord
Of the rights of the hearth and the festal board.
The sons of Priam sang
A song to the praise of the bride:
From jubilant throats they praised her then,
The bride from Hellas brought;
But now the ancient city hath changed
Her hymn to a doleful note.
She weeps bitter tears; she curses the head
Of the woe-wedded Paris; she curses the bed
Of the beautiful bride
That crossed the flood,
And filched the life of her sons, and washed
Her wide-paved streets with blood.

STROPHE II

Whoso nurseth the cub of a lion
Weaned from the dugs of its dam, where the draught
Of its mountain-milk was free,
Finds it gentle at first and tame.
It frisks with the children in innocent game,
And the old man smiles to see;
It is dandled about like a babe in the arm,
It licketh the hand that fears no harm,
And when hunger pinches its fretful maw,
It fawns with an eager glee.

ANTISTROPHE II

But it grows with the years; and soon reveals
The fount of fierceness whence it came:
And, loathing the food of the tame,
It roams abroad, and feasts in the fold,
On feasts forbidden, and stains the floor
Of the house that nursed it with gore.
A curse they nursed for their own undoing,
A mouth by which their own friends shall perish;
A servant of Até, a priest of Ruin,
Some god hath taught them to cherish.

STROPHE III

Thus to Troy came a bride of the Spartan race,

With a beauty as bland as a windless calm,
      Prosperity's gentlest grace;
And mild was love's blossom that rayed from her eye,
The soft-winged dart that with pleasing pain
      Thrills heart and brain.
But anon she changed: herself fulfilled
      Her wedlock's bitter end;
    A fatal sister, a fatal bride,
      Her fateful head she rears;
Herself the Erinnys from Jove to avenge
The right of the injured host, and change
      The bridal joy to tears.

ANTISTROPHE III

'Twas said of old, and 'tis said to-day,
That wealth to prosperous stature grown
      Begets a birth of its own:
That a surfeit of evil by good is prepared,
And sons must bear what allotment of woe
      Their sires were spared.
But this I rebel to believe: I know
      That impious deeds conspire
To beget an offspring of impious deeds
      Too like their ugly sire.
But whoso is just, though his wealth like a river
Flow down, shall be scathless: his house shall rejoice
      In an offspring of beauty for ever.

STROPHE IV

The heart of the haughty delights to beget
A haughty heart. From time to time
In children's children recurrent appears
      The ancestral crime.
When the dark hour comes that the gods have decreed,
      And the Fury burns with wrathful fires,
      A demon unholy, with ire unabated,
      Lies like black night on the halls of the fated:
And the recreant son plunges guiltily on
      To perfect the guilt of his sires.

ANTISTROPHE IV

But Justice shines in a lowly cell;
In the homes of poverty, smoke begrimed,
XVII

With the sober-minded she loves to dwell.
      But she turns aside
From the rich man's house with averted eye,
The golden-fretted halls of pride
Where hands with lucre are foul, and the praise
Of counterfeit goodness smoothly sways:
And wisely she guides in the strong man's despite
      All things to an issue of right.
Chorus.—But, hail the king! the city-taking
        Seed of Atreus' race.
How shall I accost thee! How
With beseeming reverence greet thee?
Nor above the mark, nor sinking
      Beneath the line of grace?
Many of mortal men there be,
'Gainst the rule of right preferring
Seeming to substance; tears are free
In the eye when woe its tale rehearseth,
But the sting of sorrow pierceth
No man's liver; many force
Lack-laughter faces to relax
Into the soft lines traced by joy.
But the shepherd true and wise
Knows the faithless man, whose eyes,
With a forward friendship twinkling,
      Fawns with watery love.
For me, I nothing hide. O King,
In my fancy's picturing,
From the Muses far I deemed thee,
And thy soul not wisely helming
      When thou drew'st the knife
For Helen's sake, a woman, whelming
Thousands in ruin, rushing rashly
      On unwelcome strife.
But now all's well. No shallow smiles
We wear for thee, thy weary toils
All finished. Thou shalt know anon
What friends do serve thee truly,
And who in thy long absence used
      Their stewardship unduly.

Enter AGAMEMNON *with attendants;* CASSANDRA *behind*

Aga.—First Argos hail! and ye, my country's gods,
   Who worked my safe return, and nerved my arm

With vengeance against Priam! for the gods,
Taught by no glossing tongue, but by the sight
Of their own eyes knew justice; voting ruin
And men-destroying death to ancient Troy,
Their fatal pebbles in the bloody urn
Not doubtingly they dropt; the other vase,
Unfed with hope of suffrage-bearing hand,
Stood empty. Now the captured city's smoke
Points where it fell. Raves Ruin's storm; the winds
With crumbled dust and dissipated gold
Float grossly laden. To the immortal gods
These thanks, fraught with rich memory of much good,
We pay; they taught our hands to spread the net
With anger-whetted wit; a woman's frailty
Laid bare old Ilium to the Argive bite,
And with the setting Pleiads outleapt a birth
Of strong shield-bearers from the fateful horse.
A fierce flesh-tearing lion leapt their walls,
And licked a surfeit of tyrannic blood.
This prelude to the gods. As for thy words
Of friendly welcome, I return thy greeting,
And as your thought, so mine; for few are gifted
With such rich store of love, to see a friend
Preferred and feel no envy; 'tis a disease
Possessing mortal men, a poison lodged
Close by the heart, eating all joy away
With double barb—his own mischance who suffers
And bliss of others sitting at his gate,
Which when he sees he groans. I know it well;
They who seemed most my friends, and many seemed,
Were but the mirrored show, the shadowy ghost
Of something like to friendship, substanceless
Ulysses only, most averse to sail,
Was still most ready in the yoke with me
To bear the harness; living now or dead,
This praise I frankly give him. For the rest,
The city and the gods, we will take counsel
In full assembly freely. What is good
We will give heed that it be lasting; where
Disease the cutting or the caustic cure
Demands, we will apply it. I, meanwhile,
My hearth and home salute, and greet the gods,
Who, as they sent me to the distant fray,
Have brought me safely back. Fair victory,
Once mine, may she dwell with me evermore!

Clytem.—Men! Citizens! ye reverend Argive seniors,
No shame feel I, even in your face, to tell
My husband-loving ways. Long converse lends
Boldness to bashfulness. No foreign griefs,
Mine own self-suffered woes I tell. While he
Was camping far at Ilium, I at home
Sat all forlorn, uncherished by the mate
Whom I had chosen; this was woe enough
Without enforcement; but, to try me further,
A host of jarring rumours stormed my doors,
Each fresh recital with a murkier hue
Than its precedent; and I must hear all.
If this my lord, had borne as many wounds
In battle as the bloody fame recounted,
He had been pierced throughout even as a net;
And had he died as oft as Rumour slew him,
He might have boasted of a triple coil
Like the three-bodied Geryon, while on earth
(Of him below I speak not), and like him
Been three times heaped with a cloak of funeral dust.
Thus fretted by cross-gained reports, oft-times
The knotted rope high-swung had held my neck,
But that my friends with forceful aid prevented.
Add that my son, pledge of our mutual vows,
Orestes is not here; nor think it strange.
Thy Phocian spear-guest, the most trusty Strophius,
Took him in charge, a twofold danger urging
First thine beneath the walls of Troy, and further
The evil likelihood that, should the Greeks
Be worsted in the strife, at home the voice
Of many-babbling anarchy might cast
The council down, and as man's baseness is,
At fallen greatness insolently spurn.
Moved by these thoughts I parted with my boy,
And for no other cause. Myself the while
So woe-worn lived, the fountains of my grief
To their last drop were with much weeping drained;
And far into the night my watch I've kept
With weary eyes, while in my lonely room
The night-torch faintly glimmered. In my dream
The buzzing gnat, with its light-brushing wing,
Startled the fretful sleeper; thou hast been
In waking hours, as in sleep's fitful turns
My only thought. But having bravely borne
This weight of woe, now with blithe heart I greet

Thee, my heart's lord, the watch-dog of the fold,
The ship's sure mainstay, pillared shaft whereon
Rests the high roof, fond parent's only child,
Land seen by sailors past all hope, a day
Lovely to look on when the storm hath broken,
And to the thirsty wayfarer the flow
Of gushing rill. O sweet it is, how sweet
To see an end of the harsh yoke that galled us!
These greetings to my lord; nor grudge me, friends,
This breadth of welcome; sorrows we have known
Ample enough. And now, thou precious head,
Come from thy car; nay, do not set thy foot,
The foot that trampled Troy, on common clay.
What ho! ye laggard maids! why lags your task
Behind the hour? Spread purple where he treads.
Fitly the broidered foot-cloth marks his path,
Whom Justice leadeth to his long-lost home
With unexpected train. What else remains
Our sleepless zeal, with favour of the gods,
Shall order as befits.

Aga.—Daughter of Leda, guardian of my house!
Almost thou seem'st to have spun thy welcome out
To match my lengthened absence; but I pray thee
Praise with discretion, and let other mouths
Proclaim my pæans. For the rest, abstain
From delicate tendance that would turn my manhood
To woman's temper. Not in barbaric wise
With prostrate reverence base, kissing the ground,
Mouth sounding salutations; not with purple,
Breeder of envy, spread my path. Such honors
Suit the immortal gods; me, being mortal,
To tread on rich-flowered carpetings wise fear
Prohibits. As a man, not as a god,
Let me be honored. Not the less my fame
Shall be far blazoned, that on common earth
I tread untapestried. A sober heart
Is the best gift of God; call no man happy
Till death hath found him prosperous to the close.
For me, if what awaits me fall not worse
Than what hath fallen, I have good cause to look
Bravely on fate.

Clytem.—   Nay, but my good lord will not
In this gainsay my heart's most warm desire.

Aga.—My wish and will thou shalt not lightly mar.

Clytem.—Hast thou a vow belike, and fear'st the gods?

Aga.—If e'er man knew, I know my will in this.

Clytem.—Had Priam conquered, what had Priam done?

Aga.—His feet had trod the purple; doubt it not.

Clytem.—What Priam would, thou may'st, unless the fear
    Of popular blame make Agamemnon quail.

Aga.—But popular babble strengthens Envy's wing.

Clytem.—Thou must be envied if thou wilt be great.

Aga.—Is it a woman's part to hatch contention?

Clytem.—For once be conquered; they who conquer may
    Yield with a grace.

Aga.—   And thou in this vain strife
    Must be perforce the conqueror; is it so?

Clytem.—'Tis even so: for once give me the reins.

Aga.—Thou hast thy will. Come, boy, unbind these sandals.
    That are the prostrate subjects to my feet,
    When I do tread; for with shod feet I never
    May leave my print on the sea-purple, lest
    Some god with jealous eye look from afar
    And mark me. Much I fear with insolent foot
    To trample wealth, and rudely soil the web
    Whose precious threads the pure-veined silver buys.
    So much for this. As for this maid, receive
    The stranger kindly: the far-seeing gods
    Look down with love on him who mildly sways.
    For never yet was yoke of slavery borne
    By willing neck; of all the captive maids
    The choicest flower she to my portion fell.
    And now, since thou art victor o'er my will,
    I tread the purple to my father's hall.

Clytem.—The wide sea flows; and who shall dry it up?
    The ocean flows, and in its vasty depths
    Is brewed the purple's die, as silver precious,
    A tincture ever-fresh for countless robes.
    But Agamemnon's house is not a beggar;
    With this, and with much more the gods provide us;
    And purple I had vowed enough to spread
    The path of many triumphs, had a god
    Given me such 'hest oracular to buy
    The ransom of thy life. We have thee now,
    Both root and trunk, a tree rich leafage spreading
    To shade this mansion from the Sirian dog.
    Welcome, thou double blessing! to this hearth
    That bringest heat against keen winter's cold,
    And coolness when the sweltering Jove prepares
    Wine from the crudeness of the bitter grape;

Enter the house, made perfect by thy presence.
Jove, Jove, the perfecter! perfect thou my vow,
And thine own counsels quickly perfect thou!   (Exeunt.

CHORAL HYMN

STROPHE I

Whence these shapes of fear that haunt me?
        These hovering portents why?
        Is my heart a sere inspired,
To chaunt unbidden and unhired
        Notes of dark prophecy?
Blithe confidence, my bosom's lord,
        That swayed the doubtful theme,
Arise, and with thy clear command
        Chase the vain-vexing dream!
Long years have rolled; and still I fear,
        As when the Argive band
Unloosed their cables from the shore,
And eager plied the frequent oar
        To the far Ilian strand.

ANTISTROPHE I

Now they return: my vouching eyes
        To prop my faith conspire,
And yet my heart, in self-taught hymns,
As with a Fury's burden brims,
        And will not own the lyre.
I fear, I fear: the bold-faced Hope
        Hath left my heart all drear;
And my thought, not idly tossed within,
        Feels evil creeping near.
For the heart hath scent of things to come
        And prophesies by fear;
And yet I pray, may all conspire
To prove my boding heart a liar,
        And me a foolish seer.

STROPHE II

Full-blooded health, that in the veins
        With lusty pulses hotly wells,
Shall soon have check. Disease beside it
        Wall to wall, ill-sundered, dwells.

The proud trireme, with sudden shock,
In its mid career, on a sunken rock
    Strikes, and all is lost.
Yet there is hope; the ship may rein
Its plunge, from whelming ruin free,
If with wise sling the merchant fling
    Into the greedy sea
A part to save the whole. And thus
Jove, that two-handed stores for us,
    In our mid woe may pause,
Heap gifts on gifts from yearly furrows,
And save the house from swamping sorrows,
    And lean starvation's jaws.

ANTISTROPHE II

But, oh! when black blood stains the ground,
    And the mortal mortal lies,
Shall the dead hear when thou chauntest?
    To thy charming shall he rise?
    Once there was a leech so wise
Could raise the dead, but, from the skies,
    Struck by Jove, he ceased.
But cease my song. Were link with link
In the chain of things not bound together
That each event must wait its time,
    Nor one dare trip the other,
My tongue had played the prophet's part,
And rolled the burden from my heart;
    But now, to doubt resigned,
With smothered fears, all dumb I wait
The unraveling hour; while sparks of fate
    Flit through my darksome mind.

Enter CLYTEMNESTRA

Clytem.—Come thou, too, in; this maid, I mean; Cassandra!
    For not in wrath Jove sent thee here to share
    Our family lustrations, and to stand,
    With many slaves, beside the household altar.
    Step from this car, nor bear thy spirit proudly
    Above thy fate, for even Alcmena's son,
    To slavery sold, once bore the hated yoke.
    What must be, must be; rather thank the chance
    That gave thee to an old and wealthy house;
    For they who reap an unexpected growth

Of wealth, are harsh to slaves beyond the line
Of a well-tempered rule. Here thou shalt find
The common use of bondage.

Chorus.—   Plainly she speaks;
And thou within Fate's iron toils once caught
Wert wise to go—if go thou wilt—but, soothly,
Thou hast no willing look.

Clytem.—   Nay, an' she be not
Barbarian to the bone, and speaking nought
Save swallow jabber, she shall hear my voice.
I'll pierce her marrow with it.

Chorus.—   Captive maid,
Obey! thou shouldst; 'tis best; be thou persuaded
To leave thy chariot-seat and follow her.

Clytem.—No time have I to stand without the gate
Prating with her. Within, on the central hearth,
The fire burns bright, the sheep's fat slaughter waiting,
To furnish forth a banquet that transcends
The topmost of our hopes. Wilt thou obey,
Obey me quickly! If with stubborn sense
Thou hast not ear to hear, nor voice to speak,
Answer my sign with thy barbarian hand.

Chorus.—A wise interpreter the maid demands;
Like a wild beast new caught, even so she stands.

Clytem.—Ay! she is mad; her wit to sober counsels
Is deaf; she comes from the new-captured city,
Untaught to bear the Argive bit with patience,
But foams and dashes bloody froth. I will not
Make yourself base by wasting words on her   (Exit.

Chorus.—Poor maid, I may not blame; I pity thee.
Come, leave thy seat; for, though the yoke be strange,
Necessity compels, and thou must bear it.

STROPHE I

Cass.—Ah! ah! woes me! woe! woe!
        Apollo! O Apollo!
Chorus.—Why dost thou wail to Loxias? is he
A gloomy god that he should list sad tales?

ANTISTROPHE I

Cass.—Ah! ah! woes me! woe! woe!
        Apollo! O Apollo!
Chorus.—Again with evil-omened voice she cries
Upon the god least fit to wait on woe.

STROPHE II

Cass.—Apollo! Apollo!
   My way-god, my leader Apollo!
           Apollo the destroyer!
   Thou with light labour hast destroyed me quite.
Chorus.—Strange oracles against herself she speaks;
   Ev'n in the bondsman's bosom dwells the god.

ANTISTROPHE II

Cass.—Apollo! Apollo!
   Apollo, my leader, whither hast thou led me?
          My way-god, Apollo?
   What homes receive thy captive prophetess?
Chorus.—The Atridæ's homes. This, an' thou knowst it not,
   I tell thee; and the words I speak are true.

STROPHE III

Cass.—Ha! the house of the Atridæ!
     Well the godless house I know,
   With the dagger and the rope,
     And the self-inflicted blow!
   Where red blood is on the floor,
   And black murder at the door—
     This house—this house I know.
Chorus.—She scents out slaughter, mark me, like a hound,
   And tracks the spot where she shall feast on blood.

ANTISTROPHE III

Cass.—Ay! I scent a truthful scent,
     And the thing I say I know.
   See! see! these weeping children,
     How they vouch the monstrous woe!
   Their red wounds are bleeding fresh,
   And their father eats their flesh,
     This bloody house I know.
Chorus.—The fame of thy divinings far renowned
   Have reached us, but we wish no prophets here.

STROPHE IV

   Cass.—Ha! ha! what plots she now!
     A new sorrow, a new snare
     To the house of the Atridæ,

And a burden none may bear!
A black harm to all and each,
A disease that none may leech,
And the evil plot to mar
All help and hope is far.

Chorus.—Nay now I'm lost and mazed in vain surmise.
What first she said I knew—the common rumour.

ANTISTROPHE IV

Cass.—Ha! woman wilt thou dare?
Thy bed's partner and thy mate
In the warm refreshing bath
Shall he find his bloody fate?
How shall I dare to say
What comes and will not stay?
See, to do her heart's command
Where she stretches her red hand!

Chorus.—Not yet I understand: through riddles dark
And cloudy oracles my wits are wandering.

STROPHE V

Cass.—Ha! what bloody sight is this!
'Tis a net of Hades spread—
'Tis a snare to snare her lord,
The fond sharer of her bed.
The black chorus of the place
Shout for vengeance o'er the race,
Whose offence cries for atoning,
With a heavy death of stoning!

STROPHE VI

Chorus.—What black Fury of the place
Shall shout vengeance o'er the race?
Such strange words I hate to hear.
The blithe blood, that crimson ran
In my veins, runs pale and wan
With the taint of yellow fear,
As when in the mortal anguish,
Life's last fitful glimpses languish
And Fate, as now, is near!

ANTISTROPHE V

Cass.—Ha! ha! the work proceeds!

From the bull keep back the cow!
Lo! now she seizes him
By the strong black horn, and now
She hath wrapt him round with slaughter
She strikes! and in the water
Of the bath he falls. Mark well,
In the bath doth murder dwell.

ANTISTROPHE VI

Chorus.—No prophetic gift is mine
The dark saying to divine,
But this sounds like evil quite;
For to mortal man was never
The diviner's voice the giver
Of a message of delight,
But in words of mazy mourning,
Comes the prophet's voice of warning,
With a lesson of affright.

STROPHE VII

Cass.—Fill the cup, and brim the woe!
'Tis my own heart's blood must flow
Me! miserable me!
From old Troy why didst thou bring me
Poor captive maid, to sing thee
Thy dirge, and die with thee?

STROPHE VIII

Chorus.—By a god thou art possessed,
And he raveth in thy breast,
And he sings a song of thee
That hath music, but no glee.
Like a dun-plumed nightingale
That, with never-sated wail,
Crieth Itys! Itys! aye,
As it scatters, in sweet flow,
The thick blossoms of its woe,
So singest thou to-day.

ANTISTROPHE VII

Cass.—Ah! the clear-toned nightingale!
Mellow bird, thou dost not wail,
For the good gods gave to thee

A light shape of fleetest winging,
A bright life of sweetest singing,
    But a sharp-edged death to me.

ANTISTROPHE VIII

Chorus.—By a god thou art possessed,
    And he goads thee without rest,
    And he racks thy throbbing brain
    With a busy-beating pain,
    And he presses from thy throat
    The heavy struggling note,
    And the cry that rends the air.
    Who bade her tread this path,
    With the prophecy of wrath,
    And the burden of despair?

STROPHE IX

Cass.—O the wedlock and the woe
    Of the evil Alexander,
    To his chiefest friends a foe!
    O my native stream Scamander,
    Where in youth I wont to wander,
    And was nursed for future woes,
    Where thy swirling current flows!
    But now on sluggish shore
    Of Cocytus I shall pour,
    'Mid the Acherusian glades,
    My divinings to the shades.

STROPHE X

Chorus.—Nothing doubtful is the token;
    For the words the maid hath spoken
        To a very child are clear.
    She hath pierced me to the marrow;
    And her cry of shrieking sorrow
        Ah! it crushes me to hear.

ANTISTROPHE IX

Cass.—The proud city lieth lowly,
    Nevermore to rise again!
    It is lost and ruined wholly;
    And before the walls in vain

Hath my pious father slain
Many meadow-cropping kine,
To appease the wrath divine.
Where it lieth it shall lie,
Ancient Ilium: and I
On the ground, when all is past,
Soon my reeking heart shall cast.

ANTISTROPHE X

Chorus.—Ah! the mighty god, wrath-laden,
        He hath smote the burden maiden
            With a weighty doom severe.
        From her heart sharp cries he wringeth,
        Dismal, deathful strains she singeth,
            And I wait the end in fear.
Cass.—No more my prophecy, like a young bride
        Shall from a veil peep forth, but like a wind
        Waves shall it dash from the west in the sun's face,
        And curl high-crested surges of fierce woes,
        That far outbillow mine. I'll speak no more
        In dark enigmas. Ye my vouchers be,
        While with keen scent I snuff the breath of the past,
        And point the track of monstrous crimes of old.
        There is a choir, to destiny well-tuned,
        Haunts these doomed halls, no mellow-throated choir,
        And they of human blood have largely drunk:
        And by that wine made bold, the Bacchanals
        Cling to their place of revels. The sister'd Furies
        Sit on these roofs, and hymn the prime offence
        Of this crime-burthened race; the brother's sin
        That trod the brother's bed. Speak! do I hit
        The mark, a marksman true? or do I beat
        Your doors, a babbling beggar prophesying
        False dooms for hire? Be ye my witnesses,
        And with an oath avouch, how well I know
        The hoary sins that hang upon these walls.
Chorus.—Would oaths make whole our ills, though I should
            wedge them
        As stark as ice? But I do marvel much
        That thou, a stranger born, from distant seas,
        Dost know our city as it were thine own.
Cass.—Even this to know, Apollo stirred my breast.
Chorus.—Apollo! didst thou strike the god with love?
Cass.—Till now I was ashamed to hint the tale.

Chorus.—The dainty lips of nice prosperity
    Misfortune opens.
Cass.—   Like a wrestler he
    Strove for my love; he breathed his grace upon me.
Chorus.—And hast thou children from divine embrace?
Cass.—I gave the word to Loxias, not the deed.
Chorus.—Hadst thou before received the gift divine?
Cass.—I had foretold my countrymen all their woes.
Chorus.—Did not the anger of the god pursue thee?
Cass.—It did; I warned, but none believed my warning.
Chorus.—To us thou seem'st to utter things that look
    Only too like the truth.
Cass.—   Ah me! woe! woe!
    Again strong divination's troublous whirl
    Seizes my soul, and stirs my labouring breast
    With presages of doom. Lo! where they sit,
    These pitiful young ones on the fated roof,
    Like to the shapes of dreams! The innocent babes,
    Butchered by friends that should have blessed them, and
    In their own hands their proper bowels they bear,
    Banquet abhorred, and their own father eats it.
    This deed a lion, not a lion-hearted
    Shall punish; wantonly in her bed, whose lord
    Shall pay the heavy forfeit, he shall roll,
    And snare my master—woe's me, even my master,
    For slavery's yoke my neck must learn to own.
    Ah! little weens the leader of the ships,
    Troy's leveller, how a hateful bitch's tongue,
    With long-drawn phrase, and broad-sown smile, doth weave
    His secret ruin. This a woman dares;
    The female mars the male. Where shall I find
    A name to name such monster? dragon dire,
    Rock-lurking Scylla, the vexed seaman's harm,
    Mother of Hades, murder's Mænad, breathing
    Implacable breath of curses on her kin.
    All-daring woman! shouting in her heart,
    As o'er the foe, when backward rolls the fight,
    Yet hymning kindliest welcome with her tongue.
    Ye look mistrustful; I am used to that.
    That comes which is to come; and ye shall know
    Full soon, with piteous witness in your eyes,
    How true, and very true, Cassandra spake.
Chorus.—Thyestes' banquet, and his children's flesh
    I know, and shudder; strange that she should know
    The horrors of that tale; but for the rest

She runs beyond my following.

Cass.— Thus I said;
Thine eyes shall witness Agamemnon's death.

Chorus.—Hush, wretched maiden! lull thy tongue to rest,
And cease from evil-boding words!

Cass.— Alas!
The gods that heal all evil, heal not this.

Chorus.—If it must be; but may the gods forefend!

Cass.—Pray thou, and they will have more time to kill.

Chorus.—What man will dare to do such bloody deed?

Cass.—I spake not of a man: thy thoughts shoot wide.

Chorus.—The deed I heard, but not whose hand should do it.

Cass.—And yet I spake good Greek with a good Greek tongue.

Chorus.—Thou speakest Apollo's words: true, but obscure.

Cass.—Ah me! the god! like fire within my breast
Burns the Lycéan god. Ah me! pain! pain!
A lioness two-footed with a wolf
Is bedded, when the noble lion roamed
Far from his den; and she will murder me.
She crowns the cup of wrath; she whets the knife
Against the neck of the man, and he must pay
The price of capture, I of being captive.
Vain gauds, that do but mock my grief, farewell!
This laurel-rod, and this diviner's wreath
About my neck, should they outlive the wearer?
Away! As ye have paid me, I repay.
Make rich some other prophetess with woe!
Lo! where Appolo looks, and sees me now
Doff this diviner's garb, the self-same weeds
He tricked me erst witha' live for him,
The public scorn, the sc   friends and foes,
The mark of every ribald j   r's tongue,
The homeless girl, the ravin   untebank,
The beggar'd, wretch   maniac.
And now   e prop   unmakes her,
And lea   my doom—ah   eside
My father's altar doomed to die   block
From my hot life shall drink the p   stain.
But we shall fall not unavenged: the gods
A mother-murdering shoot shall send from far
To avenge his sire; the wanderer shall return
To pile the cope-stone on these towering woes.
The gods in heaven a mighty oath have sworn,
To raise anew the father's prostrate fate
By the son's arm.—But why stand here, and beat

The air with cries, seeing what I have seen;
When Troy hath fallen, suffering what it suffered,
And they who took the city by the doom
Of righteous gods faring as they shall fare?
I will endure to die, and greet these gates
Of Hades gaping for me. Grant me, ye gods,
A mortal stroke well-aimed, and a light fall
From cramped convulsion free! Let the red blood
Flow smoothly from its fount, that I may close
These eyes in peaceful death.

Chorus.—   O hapless maid!
And wise as hapless! thou hast spoken long!
But if thou see'st the harm, why rush on fate
Even as an ox, whom favouring gods inspire
To stand by the altar's steps, and woo the knife.

Cass.—I'm in the net. Time will not break the meshes.

Chorus.—But the last moment of sweet life is honoured.

Cass.—My hour is come; what should I gain by flight?

Chorus.—Thou with a stout heart bravely look'st on fate.

Cass.—Bravely thou praisest: but the happy hear not
Such commendations.

Chorus.   Yet if death must come,
His fame is fair who nobly fronts the foe.

Cass.—Woe's me, the father and his noble children!

Chorus.—Whither now? What father and what child? Speak.

Cass.—(Approaching and starting from the house.)
Woe! woe!

Chorus.—What means this WOE? What horrid fancy scares thee?

Cass.—Blood-dripping murder reeks from yonder house.

Chorus.—How? 'Tis the scent of festal sacrifice.

Cass.—The scent of death—a fragrance from the grave.

Chorus.—Soothly no breath of Syrian nard she names.

Cass.—But now the time is come. I go within
To wail for Agamemnon and myself.
I've done with life. Farewell! My vouchers ye,
Not with vain screaming, like a fluttering bird,
Above the bush I cry. Yourselves shall know it
Then when, for me a woman, a woman dies,
And for a man ill-wived a man shall fall.
Trust me in this. Your honest faith is all
The Trojan guest, the dying woman, craves.

Chorus.—O wretched maid! O luckless prophetess.

Cass.—Yet will I speak one other word, before
I leave this light. Hear thou my vows, bright sun,
And, though a slave's death be a little thing,

Send thou the avenging hand with full requital,
To pay my murders back, as they have paid.
Alas! the fates of men! their brightest bloom
A shadow blights; and, in their evil day,
An oozy sponge blots out their fleeting prints,
And they are seen no more. From bad to worse
Our changes run, and with the worst we end. (Exit.

Chorus.—Men crave increase of riches ever
With insatiate craving. Never
From the finger-pointed halls
Of envied wealth their owner calls,
"Enter no more! I have enough!"
This man the gods with honour crowned;
He hath levelled with the ground
Priam's city, and in triumph
Glorious home returns;
But if doomed the fine to pay
Of ancient guilt, and death with death
    To guerdon in the end,
Who of mortals will not pray
From high-perched Fortune's favour far,
    A blameless life to spend.

Aga. (From within.)—O I am struck! struck with a mortal blow!
Chorus.—Hush! what painful voice is speaking there of strokes
    and mortal blows?
Aga.—O struck again! struck with a mortal blow!
Chorus.—'Tis the king that groans; the work, the bloody work,
    I fear, is doing.
    Weave we counsel now together, and concert a sure design.

1st Chorus.—I give my voice to lift the loud alarm,
    And rouse the city to besiege the doors.
2nd Chorus.—Rather forthwith go in ourselves, and prove
    The murderer with the freshly-dripping blade.
3rd Chorus.—I add my pebble to thine. It is not well
    That we delay. Fate hangs upon the moment.
4th Chorus.—The event is plain, with this prelusive blood
    They hang out signs of tyranny to Argos.
5th Chorus.—Then why stay we? Procrastination they
    Tramp underfoot; they sleep not with their hands.
6th Chorus.—Not so. When all is dark, shall we unwisely
    Rush blindfold on an unconsulted deed?
7th Chorus.—Thou speakest well. If he indeed be dead,
    Our words are vain to bring him back from Hades.
8th Chorus.—Shall we submit to drag a weary life
    Beneath the shameless tyrants of this house?